SOPRINTENDENZA ARCHEOLOGICA DI ROMA

MUSEO NAZIONALE ROMANO
PALAZZO ALTEMPS
ENGLISH EDITION

ELECTA

PALAZZO ALTEMPS

Begun by Girolamo Riario before 1477, continued by Francesco Cardinal Soderini from Volterra between 1511 and 1523, and completed by Marco Sittico Cardinal Altemps and his heirs after 1568, the construction of the palace extended with ups and downs over more than a century and a half.

Palazzo Altemps was restored by the Archaeological Bureau of Rome (part of the Ministry for Cultural and Environmental Property) in order to valorize the monument and house there the Museo Nazionale Romano's department of the history of art collecting.

In the sixteenth century, Cardinal Altemps assembled there a collection of ancient sculptures, which was subsequently broken up. The palace also housed the no longer extant Biblioteca Altempsiana, from which libraries such as the Ottoboniana and the Vatican obtained books.

The building now houses the Ludovisi Boncompagni collection, the Egyptian collection of the Museo Nazionale Romano, the Mattei collection, the sixteen remaining Altemps sculptures, and works from other collections. In consideration of the connections between the two collections, the Ludovisi collection is displayed here according to criteria similar to those adopted in the sixteenth century for the presentation of the Altemps sculptures. This allows visitors to see the antiquarian style of the sixteenth-century exhibition.

The palace stands in an area that in ancient times was occupied by marble workshops, probably in the vicinity of a temple dedicated to Apollo. In the Middle Ages, via dei Soldati ("the street of the soldiers") coincided with a patrol beat along a fortified system separating the Orsini and Colonna domains. The medieval houses were later gradually incorporated in a single building.

From the end of the nineteenth century the palace underwent major alterations, most of which were cancelled by the restoration.

*1. Palazzo Altemps
seen from Piazza
di Sant'Apollinare*

*2. View of the palace
in 1830*

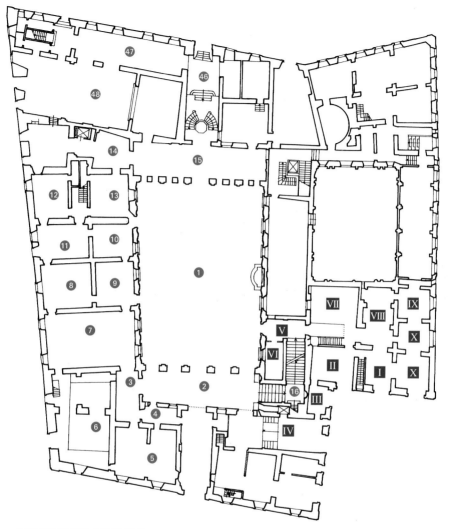

GROUND FLOOR

service areas

    I entrance and exit
   II entrance and exit, tickets, information,
       audio-guide rentals
  III entrance
  IV entrance
   V exit passageway
  VI rest rooms
 VII waiting room for groups leaving
VIII cloakroom
  IX rest rooms
   X bookshop

① Courtyard
② South arcade
③ Hall of Antoninus Pius
④ Hallway of Pluto and Zeus
⑤ Portrait room
⑥ Tower room
⑦ Herm room
⑧ Entrance hall of the Riario palace
⑨ Algardi Athena room
⑩ Athena Parthenos room
⑪ Sarcophagus room
⑫ Riario room with the Veneziani maenad
⑬ Room of Ulysses and Polyphemus
⑭ Room of Dionysius and satyr with panther
⑮ North arcade
⑯ Monumental staircase
㊻ North vestibule of the theater
㊼ Foyer
㊽ Teatro Goldoni

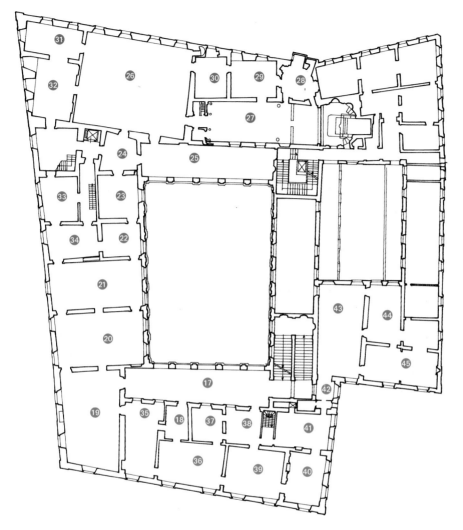

SECOND FLOOR

The Museo Nazionale Romano

The Museo Nazionale Romano was founded in 1889 in the complex of the Baths of Diocletian, where the Carthusian monastery of Santa Maria degli Angeli had risen. Over the years it has been enhanced by numerous collections acquired by the government, including the Museo Kircheriano's collections, the Boncompagni-Ludovisi sculptures and items discovered during government-sponsored excavations. Together with its counterpart in Athens, it can be considered one of the greatest archaeological museums in the world today. When the museum was founded there was discussion as to whether it was large enough for its new activity. Since then the city has grown tenfold and during that time archaeological discoveries have multiplied. The funds appropriated by special law 92 of March 23, 1981 for the conservation of Rome's archaeological heritage made it possible to start up the project of enlarging and reorganizing the Museo Nazionale Romano. In the immediate vicinity of the Museo delle Terme, a palace that had formerly housed the Collegio Massimo was recently restored to house antiquities and promote their appreciation. Both this palace and Palazzo Altemps provide new exhibition spaces, in which the archaeological objects are grouped according to their original function, provenance, excavation and collection. Another seat of the Museo Nazionale Romano is the former Planetarium, while additional exhibition spaces are currently being planned.

The Museo Ludovisi Boncompagni in Palazzo Altemps

The decision to divide the museum into several seats seems consistent with the characteristics of the city, whose archaeological heritage is spread all over. In the course of centuries, it became almost impossible to distinguish one Roman collection from another, because they were all the result of continual cross exchanges. Aristocratic collections were put together and broken up; they fluctuated between losses and replacements. The Ludovisi collection was born precisely from the first dismemberment of the Altemps. Then, in the last century, the Altemps collection was reduced to a seat with almost no statues and the Ludovisi collection to works without a seat.

In the second half of the sixteenth century Palazzo Altemps became one of the most important *diaetae statuariae*, a residence dedicated to statues and complete with a library. In light of the original function of the building and the close relationship between the two collections, there are now on display here collections of statues which it would be very difficult to exhibit according to criteria other than those originally adopted in the aristocratic palaces from which they came. Alongside what remains of the Altemps collection, works from other Renaissance and Baroque collections will be displayed in their traditional order. The latter consist mainly of the government-owned part of the Ludovisi Boncompagni collection, which in the Cesi, Orsini and Soderini collections has roots in common with the Altemps collection.

The Ludovisi collection was built partly through finds, but mainly through purchases and donations from earlier collections. On August 20, 1621 Ludovico Ludovisi bought the Altemps estate near Frascati, including several ancient statues that were part of its decoration. The Ludovisi and Altemps collections are also connected by the families' adjacent properties on the Quirinal hill: Palazzo Montecavallo (later Rospigliosi) was purchased by Giovanni Angelo Altemps and sold to Ludovisi in 1622. This sale may also have included a group of ancient sculptures.

The only Ludovisi sculptures that it has been possible to identify or propose as coming directly from the Altemps collection are at present the togaed statue with an unrelated portrait head, which has returned to the main staircase in Palazzo Altemps between the second and third floor, and the statue of Artemis, which is still on the left pillar of the entrance gate of the Casino dell'Aurora, the only building of Villa Ludovisi to escape demolition.

But since the provenance of most of the Ludovisi works is unknown, it is extremely probable that many other statues come from the Altemps collection and in the new display have returned to their original seat. For example, numerous busts generically indicated as portraits of the Caesars are documented in the deed of the sale by Altemps to Ludovisi of the Frascati estate.

Finally, there is one last affinity between the Altemps and Ludovisi collections, which can be seen in the arrangement of the new museum: both of them were divided into an antiquarian collection and a library. Like the Altemps collection, the Ludovisi one was also flanked by a "paper museum" reproducing classical objects discovered in Rome.

Façades and loggia

The façades of Palazzo
Altemps are very irregular and
asymmetrical, the result of
many alterations over time of
both the interior and exterior
of the palace, some of which
stemmed from the need to
reinforce the building.
In Piazza di Sant'Apollinare,
there are arched doorways
surmounted by the windows
of the mezzanine and, on the
right, by three small loggias.
Over the corner on the left
rises Martino Longhi the
Elder's loggia, the original
prototype of this new kind of
belvedere tower.
From Largo di Tor Sanguigna
one gets a glimpse of the first
fifteenth-century nucleus of
the palace and its tower. The
brick base, slightly inclined
with projecting footings, was
added as a reinforcement after
part of the building at the
north-west corner collapsed in
1575. On via dei Gigli d'Oro
there is a more recent façade,
as well as the narrow one of a
building incorporated in the
palace. All the façades are
decorated with coats of arms.

*3. Roof loggia. Detail
of the heraldic ibex
of Roberto Altemps*

*4. Roof loggia
of Palazzo Altemps
after the restoration*

Main entrance

The main door is framed by rustication and surmounted by a large corbel with three supporting cramp irons, which were certainly intended for a coat of arms. Beyond the door is a passageway that is the main entrance to the palace. The barrel vault is erected on two frames and near the door takes on an irregular shape because the latter, which did not have a stationary lunette, had to open towards the interior. On the sides there are a window and four doors framed by Renaissance marble cornices. The two stone benches are originals and were the models for all the others spread throughout the museum. The paving has been completely restored. A large trap door provides access to an archaeological excavation which has brought to light ancient objects, which are on display in the adjacent corner room.

In the courtyard and along the monumental staircase the marble statues of the Altemps collection still housed in the building are displayed, some of them in their original place. To these must be added the basin that constitutes the altar in the church of Sant'Aniceto.

The Altemps collection

Of the Altemps collection assembled in the sixteenth century by Cardinal Marco Sittico and enlarged by his grandson Giovanni Angelo, only sixteen works are still in the palace. Not much is known about the beginning of the collection, which was certainly assembled with both purchases and excavations. Part of it came from the Medici collection in Florence (even though the Altemps family was related to the Lombard branch of the Medici of Marignano), in particular works owned by Lorenzo the Magnificent, through the sale of the courtyard "decorations" of Palazzo Tornabuoni, later Ridolfi. Purchases were also made from the Cevoli family. Other statues may have been sold together with various land holdings, including the Frascati estate and the "vineyard" outside Porta del Popolo (which extended from the present-day Villa Borghese to Villa Giulia). On the other hand, inventories provide detailed information on the distribution of the sculptures in the rooms of the palace.
The first losses occurred in 1621, right after Giovanni Angelo Altemps's death, and coincided with the beginning of the Ludovisi collection. But until the middle of the eighteenth century the Altemps collection remained almost intact. Then came the great dispersion. At present Altemps sculptures are on display in the major museums of the world, including the Vatican Museums, the British Museum in London, the Louvre in Paris, the Pushkin in Moscow, and others in Berlin, Copenhagen, Saint Petersburg and the United States. In addition to the ancient marble statues, which have often been restored, there are also Renaissance ones. However, it is no longer possible to compile a complete list of the Altemps collection.

The Mattei collection from Villa Celimontana

The statues were formerly outside the sixteenth-century casino built by Giacomo del Duca on the Mattei estate on the *Coelimontium*, known as Villa Celimontana. An engraving of 1614 by Giacomo Lauro shows the sculptures in their original setting. The Mattei family's collection of antiquities, which had been assembled by the brothers Asdrubale and Ciriaco, was housed in three different places in Rome: the Campo Marzio palace, the *Orti Mattei* on the Palatine, and Villa Celimontana.
Once the collection had been dispersed, some of the sculptures were acquired by the government in 1923 and housed in the Museo Nazionale Romano in the Baths of Diocletian. The sculptures in Villa Celimontana recently had to be moved for security reasons and were thus added to the Mattei collection from the Museo Nazionale Romano in Palazzo Altemps.
The statues from Villa Celimontana were seriously damaged. Some heads have unfortunately been lost. Such is the case with the togaed statue, the hermaphrodite, and two statues of women, all of which date from between the first and second centuries of the Christian era and rest on ancient altars and bases, as in Villa Celimontana. The honorific base dateable to the fourth century of the Christian era is of special interest.

5. Rusticated doorway on Via di Sant'Apollinare

on the following pages:

6. The courtyard with the sculptures of the Altemps collection displayed as they originally were in the sixteenth century, under the arches of the north arcade

7. Courtyard. Detail of a pilaster on the second floor

The courtyard (1)
The courtyard was begun by Antonio da Sangallo the Elder (1513-1517), continued by Baldassarre Peruzzi and completed by Martino Longhi (1585-1589). Several coats of arms, representing the people who commissioned the work, are carved on the three stories: the ibex and the bridge struck by a lightning bolt, emblems of the family; the coats of arms of Cardinal Marco Sittico Altemps and his son Roberto; the coats of arms of the Orsini family. The four Altemps sculptures in the north arcade have been returned to their original setting. There is a fountain decorated by mosaic, paste, shells and colored gravel. With its colors, it stands out in the whiteness of the travertine and stuccowork. The most recent restoration highlighted once again the cardinal's coat of arms in the middle. It almost seems that the fountain is guarded by two herms. A small sarcophagus with season-erotes is placed in the center. The bridge struck by lightning is reproduced in color on the sides of the arch enclosing it.

The south arcade (2)

The arcade was built at the same time as the courtyard and has five arches on the short side.

On one side is the entrance to the rooms on the ground floor and on the other a staircase leading to the second floor. The two travertine archways are framed by elaborate stucco decoration portraying roses blooming on branches rising from the ground, and four rearing ibexes with enormous attributes: the Orsini and Altemps coats of arms. Between the ibexes the decoration culminates in the coat of arms of Cardinal Altemps facing that of his son Robert, which is placed over the archway leading to the staircase. In a niche there is a copy of the giant torso with stucco additions dating from the sixteenth century.

The floor of the arcade is mostly original. The lantern in the center seems to be the one Letarouilly reproduced in the nineteenth century. On display here are sculptures belonging to the Mattei collection. They come from Villa Celimontana and were urgently moved here in 1996 to prevent them from being stolen or further damaged.

The hall of Antoninus Pius (3)

Until the second half of the fifteenth century the main door of the first Riario palace was here. The large marble frame has been preserved. With the statues of Antoninus Pius (which formerly belonged to the Soderini family) and Demetra, the visit to the exhibition of the Ludovisi marbles begins.

The Boncompagni Ludovisi collection

After the Bolognese Ludovico Ludovisi, a nephew of Pope Gregory XV, became a cardinal, he built a villa on the Quirinal hill, from which there was a magnificent view of the city. On this hill, the highest in Rome, Julius Caesar had had elaborate gardens laid out around the residence he used for entertaining in the summer. The tradition of living on the hill was maintained by Sallust and several Roman emperors until, with the great palace built by Paul V, the Quirinal became the site of the popes' summer residence.
It was in this villa more than in any other property of his that Cardinal Ludovisi aimed to express his magnificence. He decorated it with paintings and a collection of ancient statues. The ancient sculptures were bought mainly from the Cesi family, while others came from the properties of the Cesarini on the Esquiline, from the Mattei, Orsini, Soderini, and Colonna, and some - among the first to be purchased - from the Altemps. The collection was enlarged with works discovered in the subsoil of the garden during the construction of the villa (the two groups of the Galatians, the acrolith), while others were purchased after their discovery elsewhere (the Ares and the Athena found in the Campo Marzio, the large sarcophagus found during excavations near San Lorenzo). The task of restoring the works and adding missing parts was entrusted by the cardinal to established sculptors such as Bernini, Ippolito Buzzi (who had already worked on the Cesi statues) and young Alessandro Algardi (who was summoned expressly from Bologna).
Around 1665 Gianbattista Ludovisi began the dispersion of marbles and paintings. The villa was subsequently acquired by Gregorio Boncompagni, from whom the Boncompagni Ludovisi family descends. The garden became an obligatory place to visit for artists and tourists, especially Germans, during their stay in Rome. It was not easy to obtain permission to enter, much less to make moulds. The latter were in great demand abroad, especially in France, but only thanks to Cardinal de Polignac was it possible to have a few executed. The fashion of copies of Ludovisi statues spread; those of Juno - Goethe's "adored Juno" - are famous. Subsequently, after studying the Ludovisi sculptures Winckelmann arrived at several interpretations that are still valid today. We know how zealously and carefully he examined the ancient marbles, to the point that he fell to the ground with the herm of Athena, luckily without damaging it.
Subsequent purchases enlarged the collection, which in the nineteenth century reached the figure of 339 sculptures, while the estate occupied an area of 74 acres. But in 1883 Prince Rodolfo Boncompagni Ludovisi sold the property to developers. The indignation expressed by international culture was unable to prevent the garden from being destroyed so that the new district could be built. Quintino Sella endeavored to save at least the most important sculptures by a special law, and thus 104 works from the seventeenth-century collection were purchased by the government in 1901.

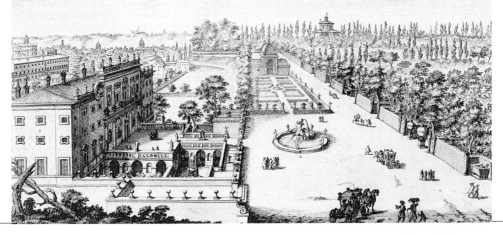

8. View of the south arcade, with the sculptures of the Mattei collection from Villa Celimontana. Next to the staircase is a copy of the colossal torso with the head of Hercules

9. Portrait statue of Antoninus Pius from the Ludovisi collection. The emperor is portrayed wearing only a cloak, with his left arm raised in the pose of an orator, while his helmet and cuirasse are resting on a support beside him

10. Idealized portrait of a veiled female figure with a large diadem, formerly identified as Demetra, from the Ludovisi collection

11. View of Villa Ludovisi at Porta Pinciana in an engraving by G. B. Falda (c. 1670). Numerous sculptures are displayed on the façade and in the garden. The herms are standing in a row on the hedge behind the fountain

**The hallway
of Pluto and Zeus** (4)
Here there was a stairway,
part of which still exists
under the trap door
at the cellar level.
Both of the heads from
the Ludovisi collection,
although known as Pluto
and Zeus, could actually
refer to Asclepius.

The portrait room (5)
The room was reduced on
the east side when the
entranceway on via di
Sant'Apollinare was built.
Now interrupted by an arch
supporting the masonry
added to the second floor, the
original vaulted ceiling was
decorated by fourteen
chamfers, nine of which have
been preserved. There are still
three flat corbels and a corner
one. In the middle was the
Riario Sforza coat of arms,
which is now off center. The
floor has been completely
restored.

On display here are portraits
from the Ludovisi collection:
Julia, Matidia, Julius Caesar,
Aristotle, Demosthenes,
Menander, a prince,
Antinous.

The tower room (6)
Built as reinforcements at the
end of the sixteenth century,
two load-bearing masonry
partitions with three arches
make three spaces out of this
large corner room, which was
added to the Riario palace
when work was carried out
after 1470. The south
portion of the vaulted ceiling
was demolished and replaced
by a wooden structure, which
was lowered just a few
centimeters during the
restoration. The original
ceiling of the room was
divided into sixteen chamfers,
of which seven are left. Three
flat corbels with a rosette and
two corner ones have also
been preserved. Remains of
constructions from the

republican and imperial eras
of ancient Rome, the Middle
Ages and more recent times
were discovered during the
excavation. On display here is
a selection of items
discovered during the
archaeological excavations
carried out in the building.

The herm room (7)
The exhibition of the
Ludovisi marbles continues
with six herms placed here
under the corbels of the ten
chamfers on the vaulted
ceiling, which was redone in
the sixteenth century. In the
center are two statues of
Apollo the Lyrist, a
decorative base and an ophite
fountain basin.

APOLLO CITAREDO

12. View of the herm room. In the foreground is an ornamental vase with ram's-head grips made in the eighteenth century utilizing ancient materials. On the sides are the twin statues of Apollo the Lyrist from the Ludovisi collection,

while in the background is one of the six herms (Athena, Hermes, Dionysius, Theseus, Hercules and a discobolus) which give the room its name

13. Statue of Apollo the Lyrist from the Ludovisi collection. The head (which was inspired by the famous one of the Apollo Belvedere), the arms and much of the left leg were restored in the seventeenth century, while the torso is

original and dates from the first half of the first century A.D.

**The entrance hall
of the Riario palace** (8)
This room corresponds to the
entrance hall of the fifteenth-
century Riario palace. One
must have entered where
there is now a window, as
indicated by the two round
eyeholes on the façade and,
inside, the irregularities on
the side of the central
chamfer. Only the bust of
Aphrodite of Cnidus (known
as Niobe) has its ancient face;
the other two Ludovisi
sculptures - the Aphrodite of
Cnidus and Demetra - have
had their heads and other
parts replaced.

The Algardi Athena room (9)
Ten chamfers divide the
greatly altered vaulted ceiling,
which was stripped of its
recently added elements
during the restoration.
When the doorway leading to
the herm room was reopened,
the walled-in embrasure and
original flooring were
discovered.
On display here is the
Ludovisi statue of Athena, of
which Algardi replaced the
head, the limbs and the
serpent's head.

The Athena Parthenos room
(10)
Much of the floor is original.
The fifteenth-century ceiling
was divided by eight chamfers.
Three rounded corbels
and two marble corner volutes
have been preserved.
The central corbel bears
the Riario rosette. The side
where the corbels are missing
is the one that was altered
in the sixteenth-century
to build the courtyard.
On display here is the statue
of the Ludovisi Athena
Parthenos, whose arms
have been restored.

The sarcophagus room (11)

The floor bears traces of repairs carried out in different periods. Ten flat corbels - six on the walls and four in the corners - support the ten chamfers on the ceiling, which still has the Riario Sforza coat of arms in the center. An interior wall of a mediaeval house, decorated with a frescoed tapestry, was discovered inside the fifteenth-century masonry. In one of the two holes that were opened in the masonry a decorated niche was also found.

The display of the Ludovisi marbles continues with a sarcophagus with a Dionysian motif surmounted by a togaed bust, the front of a sarcophagus with the feats of Hercules (reworked in ancient times with the portrait of the deceased), a muse and another statue of a woman.

The Riario room with the Veneziani maenad (12)

The stone wreath framing the Riario Sforza coat of arms stands out on the ceiling. The four rounded corbels have been preserved, as well as the four marble corner volutes. Although the floor is very worn, it is almost entirely original.

On display in the middle of the room is the maenad from the Veneziani collection. It was transferred to the Government under law 512 of 1982, which allows taxes to be paid with works of art.

The fifteenth-century staircase of the Riario palace

This staircase is the oldest one in the Renaissance palace. Only the first flight going up and a few walled-up steps of the flight that leads down to the cellars were preserved. It was restored for both regulatory and functional reasons.

The room of Ulysses and Polyphemus (13)

The cap-like vault of the room was altered when the windows were moved during the construction of the courtyard. Only three rounded corbels and marble corner volutes remain from the fifteenth century. In the center of the vault is the Riario Sforza coat of arms. Traces of Altemps coats of arms from the nineteenth century, painted in tempera, were found on the corbels. The floor is almost entirely original. The corner French window, shared with the next room, also derives from the courtyard construction work, during which a doorway between the two rooms was walled up to ensure the stability of the palace.

A fragmentary relief portraying Ulysses is on display where the now walled-up doorway used to be. In the center of the room is the original of the cyclopic torso from the Altemps collection, probably a Polyphemus or an Atlas, which was located beside the entrance to the main staircase.

14. Statue of Athena with a serpent from the Ludovisi collection. In the seventeenth century Alessandro Algardi thoroughly restored it and replaced missing parts. The attribute of the serpent allows identification of the original statue, which was discovered in the Campo Marzio near Piazza della Minerva, as a portrayal of Hygieia, daughter of Asclepius

Room of the Dionysius and satyr with panther (14)

The archway connecting the room with the enclosed space has been partially walled up. The archaeological excavation led to the discovery, at the level of the cellars, of a great variety of structures and materials going back to different periods.
The exhibition of the Ludivisi marbles continues with a colossal group of Dionysius and a satyr with a panther. Since this work belonged to the Mattei collection, it is a reminder - as is the Antoninus Pius displayed at the other end of the ground floor - of the close connection among the various collections, and in this particular case highlights the continuity between the Ludovisi and Mattei ones, which are displayed together in the adjacent north arcade. A tour of the ground floor can also begin and end with this room, from which it is easiest to reach the ground floor and the other levels.

Chiostrina

Here there was a cesspool in which a considerable amount of archaeological material has been discovered. The lights on the ground floor were reconstructed according to pictorial representations from the period when the palace was built and to fragments

discovered here. Visitors can take the elevator from here to the other floors of the building or go down to the theater from the next room.

North arcade (15)

The Dacian from the Mattei collection, formerly in the Museo delle Terme, stands between the two narrow archways that led to the Renaissance "square spiral" staircase. The latter was demolished and rebuilt at the end of the nineteenth century, and then separated with the privately owned part of the palace. At that time the second archway was also walled up. Sculptures from both the Ludovisi and Mattei collections are on display here.
Displayed in the arcade on the north side of the courtyard are other Mattei sculptures from both Villa Celimontana and the Museo delle Terme: respectively, the Republican funerary statue of "Pudicitia", that of Dionysius as Apollo Lyceus (fragmented and recomposed), and several altars with inscriptions on one side and on the other - against the background of the gallery - the Mattei Dacian in *giallo antico* marble (black in the restored parts). Also exhibited here are two *klinai*, sarcophagus lids from the Ludovisi collection, which were acquired before the rest

of the collection, at the end of the nineteenth century. In the Museo delle Terme they stood in the large ("Michelangelo") cloister and not with the other Ludovisi marbles in the small ("Ludovisi") cloister.

15. Colossal group of Dionysius and a satyr with a panther from the Ludovisi collection, a Roman replica of a Greek original from the Hellenistic age. The group was found at the Quattro Fontane on the Quirinal hill during the papacy of Sixtus V

Monumental staircase (16)

Walking back through the courtyard and the south arcade, the visitor arrives at the monumental staircase that leads up to the entrance of the Altemps library. The rooms on the third floor, which were originally occupied by the library, now house the office and documentation center of the museum. On the landing between the second and third floor there is a sculpture from the Ludovisi collection which comes from Palazzo Altemps and once again stands in its original place. Other sculptures from the Altemps collection are also displayed along the staircase: three statues, three portraits, and an oriental mask in the wall at the top. The portraits in the niches replaced sculptures of nudes, which were removed in 1897. On the second floor a haut-relief vase that is not part of the Altemps collection was recently added to the staircase.

From here the tour of the museum continues.

South loggia (17)

There is a coat of arms of Cardinal Altemps in the center of the arch the visitor goes through when coming from the staircase.
On either side is a stucco bas-relief portraying the

bridge struck by lightning. Two doors lead to the south apartment, which houses the museum's Egyptian section. At the end is the multi-marble portal leading to the rooms. On the side are two lion's paws supporting tapered pilasters ending in two volutes surmounted by two ibex heads. The architrave bears the date 1620, the ducal coat of arms of Serafino Altemps the date 1756. On the sides is another pair of coats of arms with the bridge. On the opposite side, towards the stairs, two draped female figures from the Ludovisi collection are on display where two similar sculptures from the Altemps collection once stood. Four reliefs from the Drago collection and one from the Brancaccio collection are fixed to the walls of the loggia.

Much of the del Drago family's collection comes from the Massimo collection, which was put together in the seventeenth century in the palace at the Quattro Fontane. The palace and all it contained then passed to Alessandro Albani and subsequently to the del Drago family. The four reliefs exhibited here are of

fundamental importance for the history of ancient art, because they were known and drawn as early as the fifteenth century and were subsequently made famous by Winckelmann's publications. In the sixteenth century one of the reliefs belonged to Cardinal Bruto della Valle's collection, which was housed in his palace in the Campo Marzio. The reliefs became government property in 1964 after an attempt to take them out of Italy clandestinely.

The sarcophagus with mythological scenes portrays Mars and Venus surprised by the goddess's legitimate spouse, Vulcan, who calls the gods as witnesses, according to the *Odyssey* (VIII, 325-343). It dates from 160-180 A.D. The side of the sarcophagus, which portrays a foot-bath scene with two female figures, was reproduced a number of times during the Renaissance, when it was part of the della Valle collection. It was drawn by Andrea Mantegna, copied by Raphael, and reproduced in the *Museum Cartaceum* of Cassiano del Pozzo, where there is also a drawing of a seventeenth-century marble copy of this relief, now in the

16. View of the south loggia towards the monumental staircase

17. Relief with divinities from the del Drago collection, an imperial Roman work derived from models of the Phidian school

by Zoega and by
Winkelmann, who identified
the woman as Ceres, the man
as Neptune and the horse as
their son, Arion, while the
small figure was understood
to be a guardian spirit
making libations to Neptune
"Hippius", the patron of
horses.

Jupiter seated on his throne
holding a lightning bolt,
Pluto with a cornucopia,
Persephone, Neptune with
his trident, and Anphitrites
are represented in the relief
portraying figures of gods.
The work derives from
Phidias and is thought to be
a composition of figures from
different periods, completed
at the beginning of the
second century A.D. On the
last figured slab a procession
is honoring the Dioscuri,
Castor and Pollux, and their

Louvre. In the seventeenth
century the scene was
interpreted as a preparatory
ritual foot bath before a
wedding ceremony. Modern
criticism identifies the subject
as the myth of the betrothed
Iphigenia, who realizes with
anguish that she is actually
meant to be sacrificed, but it
could also be Electra in the
myth of Orestes, on the steps
of Agamemnon's tomb (150-
170 A.D.). The piece has
been reworked numerous
times, as testified by the hole
made to adapt it for use as a
fountain and the feet of the
stool on the right, which
were executed before 1645.
In the Greek relief portraying
a funeral banquet, datable to
the fourth century B.C., the
deceased is portrayed nude,
lying on the *kline*. Beside
him are the people and
figures who were important

to him during his life. The
horse is a symbol of his social
standing, but also of the
journey into life beyond the
grave. The stylistic and
iconographic characteristics
refer to Magna Grecia.
During the neo-classical
period the relief was drawn

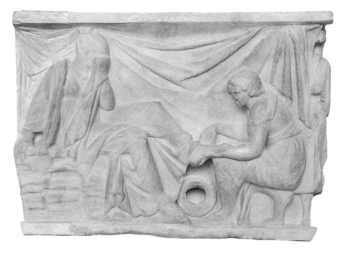

18. Greek relief
depicting a banquet
scene from the del Drago
collection

19. Side of sarcophagus
depicting a ritual foot-
bath scene from the del
Drago collection

sister, Helen, who was also born to Leda and Jupiter. This Greek relief is datable between the fifth and fourth century B.C. and was found in Rome in 1885, during construction work in the Esquiline district, on land belonging to the princes Brancaccio. They used it in their palace as decoration for the base of the "Young Bull", another extraordinary archaeological work in the Brancaccio collection, which came from the same area.

The Jandolo Venus room (18)
In this little room off the loggia there was a recently-built Egyptian-style corridor leading to the so-called D'Annunzio apartment. Pliny's passage on the presence in Rome, at the Porticus of Octavia, of a bathing Venus caused the statuary type to be attributed to the artist Diodalsas, who worked in Asia Minor in the fourth century B.C. From the period of Hadrian, this is one of the most complete ancient copies, comparable to the one in the Musei Vaticani. Like the del Drago reliefs, this work was recovered by minister Siviero during an attempt to export it illegally. Returning to the loggia, the visitor enters the painted rooms on the first floor.

The painted views room (19)
This room probably housed the chapel of the fifteenth-century palace. After that it was the main room, called the gentlemen's room, and subsequently became the main entrance to the floor. When Cardinal Altemps bought the palace in 1568, he had Vitruvio Alberi and Pasquale Cati paint a loggia in the room. The frieze with cupids standing at a balustrade is by Lattanzio Bonastri da Lucignano in Val d'Arbia. Although fragmentary, the decoration is legible. The modules - consisting of windows, false windows and groups of columns between pilasters - support a very thin entablature. The side towards the suite of rooms was painted with a blue sky framed by drapes. On the south wall in the side panel,

against a background of a wooded landscape at sunset, there is a couple in end-of-the-sixteenth-century dress. In the two central landscapes on the east wall a hunting scene is depicted on the right and a broad view with an obelisk and a large niche with lacunas on the left.
The exhibition of the Ludovisi marbles continues here: the Loghios Hermes, another statue of Mercury, a bust of a satyr on a base with bucranes on top of an altar with a modern inscription, an Asclepius, and the Lenbach Hercules.

20. View of the painted views room, with the Loghios Hermes and the Lenbach Hercules from the Ludovisi collection

21. The Loghios Hermes from the Ludovisi collection. This image of the god, who is portrayed in the pose of an orator with his right arm raised, is the result of the restoration executed in the seventeenth century by Alessandro Algardi. The sculptor added the canonical attributes of the winged headpiece, the pouch and the caduceus to the statue, but they have been removed. The original statue portrayed Hermes in his capacity as a psychopomp god, escort of the souls of the dead in the realm beyond the grave

22. View of the
painted views room,
with a gray-marble bust
of a satyr on an urn and
an altar, and a statue
of Asclepius from the
Ludovisi collection

The cupboard room (20)
This was the reception room of the fifteenth-century palace. In the accounts of the marriage of Girolamo Riario and Caterina Sforza, in 1477, ornaments are described that are similar to the decoration of the room, just as there is documentation regarding the presence in the palace of Melozzo da Forlì, to whose circle the frescoes can be attributed. On the west wall - the only well-preserved one - in front of a tapestry is portrayed a cupboard, on which the wedding gifts are laid out and the greeting cards are piled up on the sides. On the other walls there are only a few traces of the altered and damaged fifteenth-century paintings. During the building of the courtyard, the openings in the east wall were shifted, while in the second half of the sixteenth century the windows overlooking the street were enlarged upwards. The exhibition of the masterpieces of the Ludovisi collection continues in this room with the famous statue of Ares, now identified as Achilles, which was restored by Bernini; the group of Orestes and Electra; and the seated warrior.

23. Cupboard room. Fresco of the cupboard displaying the wedding gifts against a background of a floral tapestry

24. View of the cupboard room with the statue of a seated warrior

and the group of Orestes and Electra from the Ludovisi collection

25. Cupboard room. Detail of a painted capital

26. Group of Orestes and Electra from the Ludovisi collection, a work from the first half of the first century A.D. by Menelaus, an artist of the school of Praxiteles. The artist's signature is carved on the stele supporting the statue of Orestes. The name of the group derives from J.J. Winckelmann's famous interpretation: "While I was indecisively considering that group, this circumstance of the short hair suggested a new interpretation to me. It struck me that it could be Electra conversing with her brother Orestes, who was younger than her. Both of them must have had their hair cut off. Electra had hers cut by her sister Chrysothemis [...] so that she could hang it, together with the latter's, on Agamennon's tomb as a monument to their lasting grief. Orestes had done the same before revealing his thoughts to his sister". (Works, III, Book XIX, Chapter II)

27. *The Ludovisi Ares.
The sculpture is generally
considered a Roman copy
of an original from the
Hellenistic age and was
restored in 1622 by
Gian Lorenzo Bernini.
Scolars disagree on both
its identification and its
original destination.
Some believe that it
belonged to the group of
Mars and Venus in the
Temple of Mars in the
Circus Flaminius, while
others have recently
conjectured that it is the
image of Achilles from
the Temple of Neptune in
the Campus Martius*

The tales of Moses
room (21)

The room was created during
the sixteenth century by
uniting two rooms of the
Riario apartment and was
decorated by Pasquale Cati in
1591 with a frieze portraying
the ten plagues of Egypt and
the Exodus of Moses. The
episodes are painted on false
tapestries and set in elaborate
frames enlivened by standing
nudes and cupids supporting
floral festoons. Allegorical
personifications sit in false
niches at the side of the
narrative panels. Each of
them was identified by a
scroll below.
The Altemps family's coat of
arms is found in all four
corners, while those of Pius
IV and the reigning pope
appear in the center of the
external walls. On display
here is the Ludovisi throne,
which is not part of the
seventeenth-century
collection because it was
discovered during the
building of the Ludovisi
district of Rome at the end of
the nineteenth century. There
are also two colossal heads:
the archaic one of the
Acrolith and the one of Hera,
which was greatly beloved by
Goethe.

*28. View of the tales
of Moses room, with the
Ludovisi Hera in profile*

*29. Overall view of the
tales of Moses room, with
the Ludovisi Acrolith, the
Ludovisi throne
and the Ludovisi Hera*

*30. Colossal head of the
Ludovisi Hera or Juno,
one of the most famous
and admired ancient
sculptures: "to my great
joy, yesterday I placed in
my parlor a copy of the
colossal head of Juno, the
original of which is
exhibited in Villa*

*Ludovisi. It was my first
love in Rome, and now I
have it". (J.W. Goethe,*
Italian Journey, *Italian
translation, Florence,
1948, p. 183). The
sculpture was recently
identified as an idealized
portrait of Antonia
Augusta, the mother of*

*the emperor Claudius,
who was deified by her
son after her death and
extolled as an unsurpassed
example of marital virtue
and maternal dedication*

"Then, as soon as he (Cronos) had cut off his [father Uranus's] genitals and hurled them from the mainland into the stormy sea, the latter were carried out to sea for a long time and all around white foam sprang from the immortal flesh. In that foam a young girl was formed. At first she stayed on holy Cythera, and then went away from there and reached Cyprus surrounded by the waves of the sea. Thus a goddess full of grace and charm came out, and grass grew under her shapely feet. The gods and men call her Aphrodite (the goddess born out of foam, Cytherea of the beautiful crown) because she was raised in foam. They also call her Cytherea, since she stayed on Cythera, as well as Cyprogenea, because she was born on Cyprus surrounded by the waves of the sea, and also Philomnedes for having risen from the genitals". (Hesiod, Theogony, 188-200)

31. The Ludovisi throne.

on the preceding pages: frontal relief portraying the birth of Aphrodite Urania as she comes out of the sea foam fertilized by the genitals of Uranus (which were cut off by Cronus) and is welcomed on land by two Horae

on these pages: lateral relief with a female figure sprinkling incense over a flame and nude female figure playing the flute. Stylistic and iconographic characteristics, together with excavation data, have allowed the work to be identified as an original from the Greek colonies in Italy, datable to the middle of the fifth century B.C. and part of the furnishings of the Aphrodite sanctuary at Locri Epizefiri, on the Ionic coast of Calabria. Indeed, there is also other evidence proving the presence at Locri of the myth, cult and iconography of Aphrodite Urania. The goddess had a turtle shell under her foot, alluding to the

celestial vault, portrayed
by Phidias in the Greek
sanctuary at Elis. Fictile
pinakes *are evidence
of both the moment
of the goddess's birth
from the waves of the sea
and the one right after
that when Aphrodite
is welcomed and dried*

*by the Horae. The
Ludovisi throne was
discovered at the end of
the nineteenth century
on the grounds of Villa
Ludovisi. Its presence in
Rome has been
connected with the
republican temple of
Venus of Eryx at Porta*

*Collina, which
subsequently may have
been incorporated in the
Horti of Julius Caesar,
who had proclaimed
himself a direct
descendant of the Trojan
Venus of Eryx.
Still debated are the
conjectures about its*

*connection with its twin,
the Boston throne, as
well the exegesis and
authenticity of the reliefs
of the latter*

The four-seasons antechamber (22)

The small room is decorated with a frieze attributed to Antonio Viviani. Extremely common at the end of the sixteenth century, the decorative pattern presents small fantastic landscapes in panels framed by grotesques, together with allusions to the passing of time. In the center of each wall there is a medallion with the personification of a season, while animals are depicted in the upper part of the frieze. On display here are two heads and a fragmentary relief from the Ludovisi collection: Heracles, Juno, and the myth of Phedra.

The Cardinal's bedroom (23)

This room was chosen as their bedroom by the lords of the palace in several periods. Only in the seventeenth century did it become Duke Pietro Altemps's audience room. The ceiling and the upper part of the wall plastering are from the fifteenth century. The frieze below the ceiling, with landscapes, grotesques and coats of arms, dates from the middle of the sixteenth century and was cut to make room for a frieze with battle scenes painted in tempera in the seventeenth century by Francesco Allegrini after drawings by Antonio Tempesta. By making the various phases visible, the room documents the succession of the different periods in the history of the palace, its inhabitants and their taste.

On display here from the Ludovisi collection are the *rosso antico* Dionysiac masks, the busts of Hygieia and Attis, and the fragmentary relief portraying the judgement of Paris. The parts that Algardi made in stucco for the latter were removed after it was acquired by the Government and their whereabouts is still unknown.

32. *The Cardinal's bedroom with the busts of Hygieia and Attis and the relief portraying the judgement of Paris from the Ludovisi collection*

33. Rosso antico *marble relief with a Dionysiac mask from the Ludovisi collection. The presence of the two holes proves that it was part of the decoration of a fountain*

The Mercy study (24)
On the ceiling of this room scenes from the life of the Virgin are represented in gilded and painted stucco frames. The painting was executed by Vitruvio Alberi in 1590, while the stucco work is by Pompeo dell'Abate and Stefano Furcheri. In the center of the ceiling is portrayed the Madonna of Mercy, amid scenes from the life of Mary. In the corners there are four large stucco Altemps coats of arms, together with allegorical figures.
A base with relief portraying winged dancers, from the Ludovisi collection, is in the center of the room.

The painted loggia (25)
The loggia housed numerous statues from the Altemps collection, including the portraits of the twelve Caesars. It was decorated like a secret garden of delights. Commissioned by Marco Sittico Altemps just before 1595, the year of his death, the decoration shows a taste for opulence and the exotic. Not only the animals, but also the fruits adorning the arbor, such as the pineapple, are ones that had been discovered during geographical explorations and had just been imported from the New World. The wall on the study side is decorated with two landscapes, which are probably by Cati or Alberi, or both. The decoration of the lunette with heraldic motifs is by Antonio Viviani, while the one with putti playing with an ostrich derives from Raphael. The ceiling is decorated with a continuous arbor divided into different spheroidal vaults painted with an extremely refined illusionary technique. Adorned by marbles, stucco work and paste mosaics, the fountain dates from 1594.
Displayed here much as they were by the Altemps themselves - on two Renaissance bases and ten restored ones - are the so-called twelve Caesars from the Ludovisi collection, in addition to inscribed bases and altars.

34. View of the painted loggia, with the fountain and the portraits of the Caesars from the Ludovisi collection

35. *The painted loggia.*
Detail of the fountain
with three little fauns

36. The painted loggia.
Detail of the ceiling
decorated with arbors

The fireplace salon (26)
This room for entertaining
was created by Martino
Longhi the Elder, who also
designed the fireplace, after
the northwest corner of the
palace collapsed in 1575 and
Marco Sittico Altemps
ordered all the structures of
that part to be completely
rebuilt. Thus this
extraordinarily large room
was created to serve as a
picture gallery and a place to
hold parties. One can infer
what was in the room along
with the monumental
fireplace and the Altemps
sarcophagus from inventories
and a floor plan from 1798.
The fireplace remained where
it was originally until 1873,
when it was sold and moved
elsewhere. Recently it was
returned to its original place
and restored.
Here, too, the Altemps
arrangement is followed quite
closely. The place of the
Altemps sarcophagus has
been taken by the so-called
Grande Ludovisi sarcophagus,
on which the bust of Mars is
traditionally placed. In the
center of the room are the
group of the suicide Galatian
and his wife, an ancient
marble copy of the
Pergamene bronze of which
the dying Galatian in the
Musei Capitolini was also a
part, and a female figure,
whose face is thought to be
reproduced in the head of the
Ludovisi Erinys.

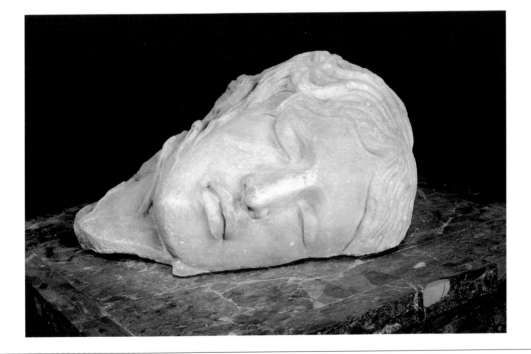

*37. The fireplace salon,
with the suicide
Galatian from the
Ludovisi collection*

*38. The Ludovisi Erinys,
frontal view*

39. The group of the suicide Galatian from the Ludovisi collection. The sculpture was found, together with the one of the dying Galatian now in the Musei Capitolini, in the seventeenth century during the construction of Villa Ludovisi on land that in antiquity had been occupied by the sumptuous estate that belonged first to Julius Caesar and later to Sallust, called the Gardens of Sallust. A recent study has shown that, together with a third one portraying a wounded woman with a baby at her breast, the two sculptures belonged to a single group of bronzes commissioned by Attalus I, king of Pergamum, to decorate the Sanctuary of Athena Nikephoros ("victory bearer") and commemorate his victory over the Galatians. The marble Roman copy was commissioned by Julius Caesar to celebrate his victory over the Gauls and placed by the dictator in the garden of his estate on the Quirinal Hill

40. *The fireplace salon.
Monumental fireplace
of Cardinal Marco
Sittico Altemps*

41. *The fireplace salon.
Caryatid on the
architrave of the fireplace
with the heraldic ibex
head*

42. Monumental
Grande Ludovisi
sarcophagus with battle
scenes. Organized
on three levels, the
frontal reliefs portray the
victors in the upper part,
the combatants in the
center, and the
vanquished in the lower
part. Among the victors,
the warrior whose
forehead is marked by a
cross-seal has been
identified as Hostilian,
son of the emperor
Decius, who died
in 252 A.D.

43. Relief portraying the
helmeted head of the god
Mars, to which the bust
was added in the
sixteenth century.
Formerly known as
"Pirrus", it reflects the
iconography of Mars
Ultor in the Forum of
Augustus and dates from
the beginning of the
second century A.D.

The church of Sant'Aniceto (27)

The church dedicated to Saint Anicetus, pope and martyr, is traditionally listed among the main ones of Rome, because, to be sure, of its extraordinary opulence, but also because of its unique privilege of housing in a private residence, amidst a large number of relics, the remains of Saint Anicetus, one of the first popes.

The church was commissioned by Giovanni Angelo Altemps in 1603. The stucco work was executed by Nicolò Carabello Muratore. The dome was already completed in 1607, and the church was inaugurated on October 28, 1617, with the translation of the remains of Saint Anicetus. In 1618 the painting by Ottavio Leoni in the *confessio*, the marble inlays in the presbytery, gilt decorations, furnishings and other finishing works were executed.

The discovery of an account of the death of Roberto Altemps, who was sentenced by Sixtus V to beheading for adultery, made clear the influence of this capital sentence - endured by the family, but considered unjust - on the subsequent artistic production, and in particular on the iconography of the church. As a reminder of his unheeded entreaties, the victim's father devoted himself

to the cult of Mercy, while his son, Giovanni Angelo - who was born an orphan on Saint Anicetus's feast day - altered the story of the saint's life. After the discovery of a tomb on the via Appia, Giovanni Angelo invented Anicetus's martyrdom by beheading. He commissioned a church in the style of those dedicated to Saint Philip Neri and had the walls decorated with two cycles dedicated to

Saint Anicetus, which can be interpreted as an allegory of the family's vicissitudes. The large one, which is in the central part of the church, is the work of Antonio Cirignani, called Pomarancio. Above the cornice there is the procession with the instruments of torture. On the ceiling - which is decorated with the cross, the sword, the pontifical keys, and four ribbons inscribed in

44. Church of Sant'Aniceto. Interior

45. Church of Sant'Aniceto. Altar

on the following page:

46. Church of Sant'Aniceto. Presbytery. Panels with marble inlays from the beginning of the seventeenth century

gold and supported by angels - is portrayed the glory of Saint Anicetus, probably the work of Polidoro Mariottini. Next to the large arch there is a hole with a gilded grating to allow the music and singing from the music room above to be heard.

Framed by the two evangelist patrons of Marco Sittico and Giovanni Angelo, the presbitery is decorated with scenes dedicated to the Virgin Mary. They, too, can be interpreted with reference to the vicissitudes of the Altemps family.

The apse houses the reliquary, dated 1612. The complete list of relics is engraved on two slabs of black limestone. The remains of Saint Anicetus lie in the altar font, behind which is the *confessio*. Here is the second cycle of stories about Saint Anicetus, an oil mural painted by Ottavio Leoni. Saints Zosimo and Famiano were added in 1766. On the ceiling of the presbytery, amidst angels near the arch where the central part of the church begins, two winged putti carry the ducal crown or that of the martyrdom. In the middle there is a portrait of the Virgin Mary.

On the altar is a free modern copy in oil of the Trastevere icon, Our Lady of Mercy. On the balcony above the entrance is a recent portrait of Saint Cecilia.

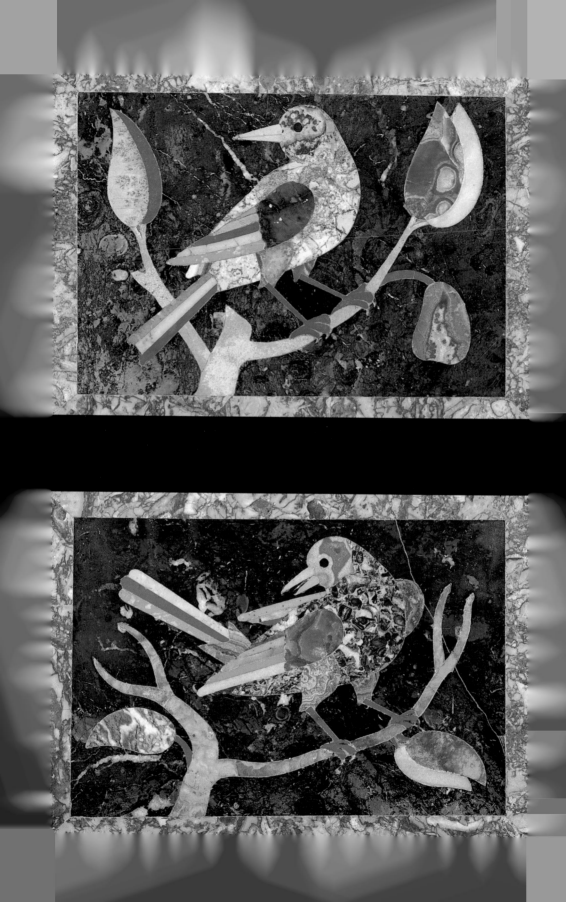

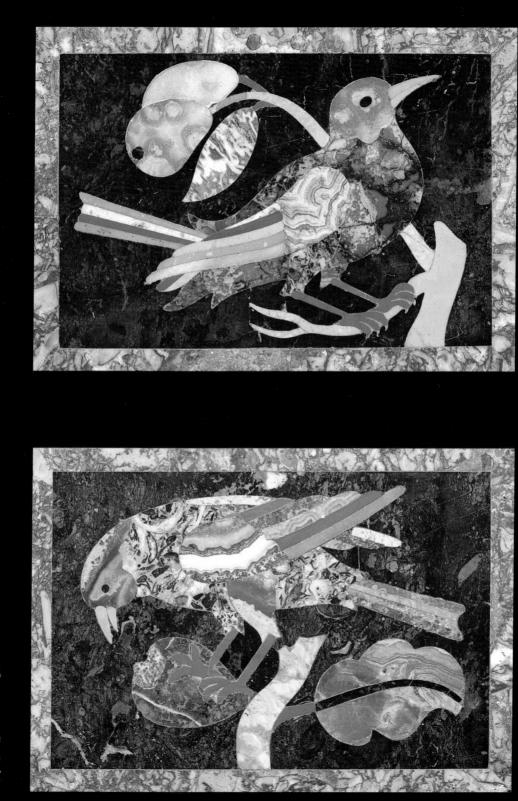

47. Church
of Sant'Aniceto. Detail
of the painted ceiling
depicting a procession
of angels in glory with
palm branches

48. Church
of Sant'Aniceto. North
wall with images of the
saint's martyrdom
executed by Antonio
Cirignani in the first
decades of the
seventeenth century. In
the center is the pope,
Saint Anicetus, just
before his beheading; on
the left Christ on
Calvary; and on the
right a compassionate
woman gathering the
martyr's blood

49. Church
of Sant'Aniceto. Wood
ceiling of the confession
behind the altar,
decorated with mother-of-
pearl flowers

on the following page:

50. Church
of Sant'Aniceto.
The sacristy door

The octagonal chapel (28)
Begun by Cardinal Marco
Sittico, it was completed by
his grandson Giovanni
Angelo as a provisional
chapel to use while work was
being done to enlarge the
main chapel and transform it
into a church. Paid for on
April 10, 1608, the lantern
has a ceiling decorated with a
haut-relief glory of martyrs.

The sacresty (29)
In 1614 the carpenters
Giovan Pietro Acciari and
Lorenzo Modesti were paid
for the walnut piece of
furniture. Especially
interesting is the secret of the
lock, which allowed
numerous bolts to be moved
in different directions with a
single turn of the key, as in a
modern safety lock.
The Altemps coat of arms is
in the middle of the ceiling.

**The chapel of Saint Charles
Borromeo** (30)
Original sixteenth-century
tapestries are kept here; a
velvet and leather one from
Mantua is displayed on the
walls. In the case on the altar
is a fragment of a chasuble
thought to be Saint Charles
Borromeo's. The coat of arms
of Cardinal Altemps is on the
ceiling. The manuscript
volumes of music in the
display cases contain
autograph scores expressly
composed for the Altemps

chapel at the end of the
sixteenth century and the
beginning of the seventeenth.

**The room of the *Piccolo
Ludovisi* sarcophagus** (31)
There is an autograph
drawing by Martino Longhi
of this room. The
extraordinary thickness of the
masonry is the result of the
work carried out in 1575 to
reinforce the palace. The only
sixteenth-century flooring
still preserved on the second
floor was discovered under a
series of floors resting on
each other.
The exhibition of the
Ludovisi marbles continues
here with the so-called
Piccolo Ludovisi sarcophagus
depicting a Roman victory,
two reliefs, a togaed statue
and an inscribed base.

51. Room with the
Piccolo Ludovisi
sarcophagus.
*In the foreground is
a detail of the sarcophagus
relief depicting a battle
between Romans and
barbarians datable to the
last decades of the second
century A.D.*

The obelisk room (32)

Fragmentary frescos depicting obelisks were discovered near the northwest corner. Given their location, which is specified in the payments, they must be the works for which Gaspare Pittore, perhaps Memberger, was paid in 1580 and 1581. Nevertheless, the decorations preserved in the window embrasures could even be work that survived the collapse in 1575. In effect, Cardinal Altemps commissioned numerous works right after he bought the palace in 1568.

The subjects presented by the Ludovisi marbles displayed here fundamentally match those of the Altemps ones placed across from the chapel, emphasizing the contrast with Dionysian or erotic themes. Exhibited here are the Dadophorus, the group with Pan and Daphne and the one with satyr and nymph, and two muses: Calliope and Urania.

The Duchess's room (33)

This room was the private parlor of Duchess Isabella Lante Altemps, who married Duke Pietro in 1636. The frieze with mythological episodes was painted by Giovanni Francesco Romanelli in 1654. On display here are the Ludovisi statues of Aphrodite bathing and Cupid and Psyche, which match the subjects portrayed in the frieze.

The Duchess's antechamber (34)

On the west wall at the level of the floor two medieval frescoed niches were discovered, which are similar in their decoration to those that can be seen in the room below. On the north wall is a fragment of a fifteenth-century frieze with palmettos. The ceiling is also from the fifteenth century.

On display here are the remains of the frieze by Polidoro Caldera and Maturino da Firenze, which was detached from the exterior façades. The statues of Aphrodite bathing and the child with a goose had been unified in the Ludovisi collection to compensate for the absence of the group with Leda and the swan. The twisted column, which foreshadows the Bacchic themes, rests on the altar of Cecilio Gorgonio.

The Bacchus room (35)
The room had been divided into two parts. On the ceiling an illusionary wood decoration executed in oil and enamel paint conceals the remaining Renaissance decorations, which have been uncovered only in a strip where the partition used to be. The paintings exhibited here were glued on the walls and partitions of an adjoining room, which had been created by dividing the painted-views room.
Two sides in relief of the sarcophagus depict the myth of Jason and the scene of *dextrarum iunctio*. In addition to the pouring satyr and the Dionysius with a panther, on display here is a completely modern statue of Dionysius, which testifies to the taste for imitations of antique art. In a corner there is a column.
The exhibition of the Ludovisi collection ends with an archaic Egyptian bust, a shepherd king, which provides an introduction to the Egyptian collection of the Museo Nazionale Romano.

**The room
of the Bull Api** (36)
This room is particularly interesting from the point of view of the restoration. In most of the other rooms the Renaissance paintings were concealed by simple, uniform color washing, while here

there were real decorations, which - even though they were recent - posed the problem of choosing which period to favor in the final presentation.
With regard to the Egyptian material, it was thought appropriate to present three thematic sections, each of which sums up an aspect of the reception by the West of the civilization of the Pharaohs.
The first section is dedicated to political theology: from the myth of Osiris and the foundation of the cult of Serapis and dynastic worship to the gradual ufficialization by the Romans of the Alexandrine divinities for programmatic and propagandistic purposes.
The second section, dedicated to popular worship, presents the unofficial aspects of religion in the West, organized by divinity

(Serapis, Isis, Isis-Itathor, Arpocrates).
The third section, on places of worship in Rome, presents material from several important temple complexes. This section consists mainly of the sculptures found in the Iseo Campense (Piazza Sant'Ignazio) and ends with the most significant items from the Syrian sanctuary on the Janiculum.
Writing at length about Egypt in the second and third book of his *History*, Herodotus dwells on the bull Api. In the second book he writes as follows:
The master of all of Egypt, Psamtik built for Ephesto the south-facing propylaea of Memphis, and across from the propylaea built a courtyard for Api - all enclosed by columns and full of figures - where Api is kept when it appears.
Instead of columns as supports, in the courtyard there are

55. Statue of Aphrodite bathing, attended by an erote holding her towel. The Roman copy from the imperial age reproduces a third-century-B.C. bronze original, famous in antiquity, by Diodalsas.

56. View of the Bacchus Room. In the foreground is the Pouring Satyr, a replica of the famous work by Praxiteles from the fourth century B.C. and further in, on the left, the seventeenth-century Dionysius. Both are from the Ludovisi collection

*enormous statues 10 cubits tall.
Api corresponds to Epaphus in
the language of the Hellenes.*
(Herodotus, *History*, II, 153).
In the third book he
describes the wounding and
death of Api. The diorite
statue of Api, also called the
Brancaccio Bull after the
collection from which it
comes, was for many years on
loan from Rome to the
Museo Egizio in Turin
because of the lack of suitable
exhibition space in the
capital. The hind part has
been restored. The original
fragment, transformed into
an ashtray, belongs to the
Museo Barracco.
Also displayed in the room is
a relief from Ariccia, which
presents another depiction of
the bull Api. On one side of
the relief is a small statue of
Isis and on the other a
headless little statue of a
priestess. Other works
displayed here are a statue of
a pharaoh, the head of an
Isiac priest, and one of a
young boy.

The Syrian-idol room (37)
This room is part of what the
inventories call Carlo
Borromeo's, and subsequently
Cornelia Orsini's, apartment.

Except for the wood ceiling,
it is not decorated.
Exhibited here are a
Dionysius with traces of
gilding, a statue of Atargatis,
Jupiter on a throne Hadad-
style, the group of the Horae,
an altar, and a display case
with the Syrian idol from the
Janiculum.

**The painted-tabernacle
room** (38)
On the wall is an incomplete
decoration: a small,
Oratorian-style altar with a
tabernacle in the form of a
cabinet like those on display
in the Sala d'Ercole on the
Capitoline.
The exhibition of the
Egyptian collection continues
here with two portrait heads,
a marble wig, an altar, and a
candelabrum.

**The Behbeit el-Hagar
temple-relief room** (39) The
issues that have already been
touched upon regarding the
restoration of other rooms
also had to be faced in this
one. The ceiling is the result
of a recent transformation.
The absence of preceding
phases concealed by the latest
one led to the decision to
restore the recent alteration.

With regard to the frieze
adorned with trophies,
however, it was decided to
recover the preceding phase,
preserving the latest one only
in those places where it
covered up gaps in the older
painting.
On display here in addition
to the temple relief from
Behbeit el-Hagar (*Isidis
oppidum*) are a lion and a
sphinx (both of which are
fragmentary), a base with the
feet of a statue, the torso of a
pharaoh, and the head of a
Isiac priest, which introduces
the Isiac theme illustrated in
the next room.

**The so-called
D'Annunzio room** (40)
With its false marbles and
elaborate wood, fabric,
mirror and stucco
decorations, the so-called
D'Annunzio room is the only
one whose eighteenth-
century forms have been
preserved. The four stucco
figures placed above the two
doors may be the ones
executed in 1686 by
Francesco Bogi. The panels
between the wood pilasters
were adorned by bandy
tapestry, which was
subsequently replaced by
damasks.
The imprints of various later
restorations were discovered
in the bedding mortar under
the recent flooring. The
original fishbone pattern was

adopted in the recent restoration. On the plaster concealed by the tapestries over the fireplace the sketch of a chandelier was discovered, which influenced the choice of the main lighting source.
On display here are a statue of Isis and the head of an Isiac priestess.

The cosmography antechamber (41)

This antechamber probably corresponds to the space indicated in the inventories as the cosmography and map room. In the sixteenth century, Giovanni Antonio da Varese (called Vanosino), a cosmographer painter, was paid for paintings with geographical and astrophysical decorations. Thus the absence of traces of decorations on the walls is not an element of uncertainty in this case, but is consistent with the presence of the paintings and thus with the identification of the room.
The section dedicated to the Egyptian collection of the Museo Nazionale Romano ends here with the bas-relief from the Ptolemaic period with an almost engraved profile, the regal couple of Nero as Pharaoh (one of the two figures is much smaller than the other and is barely discernible), a statue of Serapis seated, and the head of an Isiac priest.

Entrance hallway to Roberto Altemps's apartament (42)

The license issued by the building commissioners for enlarging the corner of the palace by ten and a half palms - making Piazza Sant'Apollinare smaller - dates from 1583. Thus only after that date was work begun on the apartment destined for Roberto Altemps, who must not have ever lived in it, however, considering his forced stay in Avignon and - after his return to Italy - his sentencing to death in 1586. On the exterior, the corner is made of plaster rather than stone. Tomographic examination has revealed traces of decoration with a canopied arbor on the vaulted roof and false windows in the lunettes.
Displayed here is the Mattei herm, which introduces the provenance of the sculptures exhibited in the large room connected to this small entrance hall.

The portrait salon (43)

Between 1724 and 1732 Palazzo Altemps was inhabited by Melchior de Polignac, ambassador of Louis XV, who set up the picture gallery in this large room. Since the walls were used to hang paintings, they were obviously not decorated. Only more recently, after the room had been split up, were several of them decorated with an architectural motif with pilasters, which was partly recovered in the restoration.
In 1923 the Italian Government acquired numerous sculptures from the large collection that Ciriaco Mattei had assembled in the seventeenth century in his villa on the Celian hill. They were housed in the Museo Nazionale Romano in the Baths of Diocletian and bought to Palazzo Altemps from Villa Celimontana for security reasons. Some of these sculptures are documented by eighteenth-century engravings. Displayed here are six reliefs, including the funerary relief, with a dedication to Anteros and Myrsine, which was found near Santa Maria Sopra Minerva; two other funerary reliefs, one from the republican age and the other from the second century A.D.; the front of a fragmentary sarcophagus from the Antonine age with images of the myth of the origin of Rome; and two reliefs with a trophy and a sacrificial scene.
A series of six heads and two busts portrays emperors, philosophers and mythological heroes. A composite capital with decorations and winged victories, which stylistically belongs to the age of Constantine, comes from the Baths of Caracalla.

57. Room of the bull Api. The so-called Brancaccio Bull, after the name of the original collection.

on the following pages:

58-59 The hot-bath room. Details of the frescoed decoration, with landscapes referring to the months and seasons of the year

In the middle of the room is the display table for coins made for King Vittorio Emanuele II - a collector of ancient coins - which now belongs to the Italian government. On the round top are revolving metal plates for examining and cataloguing the coins, while the numismatics books and catalogues needed for such examination were housed on a large revolving circular shelf in the middle of the table, which is furnished with four chairs.

The hot-bath room (44)
Pasquale Cati and Vittorio Alberi painted the frescoes adorning this room. They were severely damaged in recent times. On the floor can be seen the pipes for the steam baths and the three separate systems serving the *calidarium* (in the middle), *tepidarium* and *frigidarium*.

Rooms of Roberto Altemps's apartment (45)
In two of the three rooms of Roberto Altemps's apartment, which are connected by large archways, the original ceilings were discovered. They had long been concealed by double ceilings. On the walls a complex series of re-paintings of these room was discovered.
Redescending the staircase and walking across the courtyard, the visitor reaches the north vestibule of the theater, which can also be entered from the door on Vicolo dei Soldati.

North vestibule of the theater (46)
During work carried out by the Pontificio Collegio Spagnolo, the octagonal marble parapet of a well was moved here from its original location in the courtyard of

"the jewel". It was executed in 1585 by the stonecutter Stefano di Francesco del Zoppo. Sculpted coats of arms of Cardinal Marco Sittico alternate with the bridge and ibex emblems. At the sides of the curved ramps of the staircase are two large alabaster jugs. All the other decorations of the entrance hall date from the last years of the nineteenth century. Two panels with vegetal motifs adorn the vaults. Above the north entrance is painted a trophy with a mask, two volumes of works by Goldoni and Alfieri, various instruments and a scroll.

The foyer (47)
The foyer was decorated by Ettore Cretoni. The vaulted ceiling is painted in the manner of Pietro Ridolfi. In the center are portrayed three

draped putti with a vine shoot adorned with roses. The two lunettes are decorated with pairs of monochromic satyr musicians, while three wood chandeliers hang from the ceiling.

The Teatro Goldoni (48) The palace houses one of the oldest private theaters in Rome. It is located at the northwest corner of the building, which was rebuilt after it collapsed in 1575, with the creation of large rooms on both the ground and second floors. The new room on the ground floor, however, was initially occupied by the stable, and only later was the theater described. In 1870 it was mentioned among the theaters of Rome with the name of "Goldoni". On September 26, 1886 the Altemps-Goldoni was renamed Teatro Romanesco. Along with the palace, it became the property of the Holy See in 1887. Subsequently the rooms were completely restored according to the project of the architect Francesco Vespignani, the work being carried out under the direction of the architect Valentino Grazioli. The decorations were executed by Ettore Cretoni, while the tragic and comic masks on the ceiling of the theater were painted by Gioacchino Pagliei. The theater was inaugurated on June 21, 1890, and in 1898 was endowed with a gallery and became the seat of the Società Filodrammatica Romana.

As early as 1905 this theater was used as a projection room, first for the magic lantern and later for one of the first motion picture projectors. It was subsequently used until 1985 as a piano bar under the name Old Goldoni. From the theater one can return to the rooms on the ground floor through the room with the Dionysius and a satyr with a panther or, walking across the courtyard, visit the palace stable through the door to the right of the fountain. Leaving on the right the ramp under the staircase leading to the cellar, one first enters the original kitchen of the palace, which looked out onto the courtyard of the jewel, and then the stable, which was later transformed into shops and now houses the museum's various supplementary services. Then one returns to Piazza di Sant'Apollinare.

BIBLIOGRAPHY

B. Palma, *I Marmi Ludovisi: Storia della Collezione*, in A. Giuliano (edited by), *Museo Nazionale Romano. Le sculture*, I, 4, Rome 1983.

B. Palma, L. de Lachenal, *I Marmi Ludovisi nel Museo Nazionale Romano*, in A. Giuliano (edited by), *Museo Nazionale Romano. Le sculture*, I, 5, Rome 1983.

B. Palma, L. de Lachenal, M. E. Micheli, *I Marmi Ludovisi dispersi*, in A. Giuliano (edited by), *Museo Nazionale Romano. Le sculture*, I, 6.1, Roma 1986.

F. Scoppola (edited by), *Palazzo Altemps. Indagini per il restauro della fabbrica Riario Soderini Altemps* (LSA 8), Roma 1987.

A. Giuliano (edited by), *La collezione Boncompagni Ludovisi. Algardi, Bernini e la fortuna dell'antico*, catalogo della mostra (Rome, December 1992 - April 1993), Rome 1992.

F. Scoppola, *Influssi della "giustizia" sistina sulla produzione artistica successiva: il restauro della cappella della Madonna della Clemenza e di S. Aniceto in palazzo Altemps* , in M. Fagiolo, M. L. Madonna (edited by),

Sisto V. I, Roma e il Lazio, Proceedings of the Sixth International Course on High Culture, Accademia Nazionale dei Lincei (Rome 1989), Rome 1993, pp. 619-664.

G. Carbonara, *Palazzo Altemps in Roma: ricerche e restauri*, "Tema, tempo materia architettura", 1, 1993, pp. 8, 9, 10.

G. Croci, F. Scoppola, *Il restauro di Palazzo Altemps* , "Tema, tempo materia architettura", 1, 1993, pp. 12 ss.

P. Petraroia, *Palazzo Altemps: la lettura delle superfici pittoriche*, "Tema, tempo materia architettura", 2, 1993, pp. 14-18.

F. Scoppola (edited by), *Il sistema museale romano. Palazzo Altemps. Restauri e allestimento*, "Il Museo", 3, 1994, pp. 1-52.

M. De Angelis d'Ossat, *I rilievi Massimo-del Drago del Museo Nazionale Romano in palazzo Altemps*, in *Camillo Massimo collezionista di antichità. Fonti e materiali*, "Xenia Antiqua", 3, Rome 1996, pp. 205-212.

F. Scoppola, *Sant'Aniceto e Beata Vergine della Clemenza in palazzo Altemps - Giustizia papale e clemenza divina*, in *"Roma sacra, guida alle chiese della città eterna"*, II, 7, 1996, pp. 58-64.

Il Trono Ludovisi e il Trono di Boston, Proceedings of the Conference (Venice, September 12, 1996), "Quaderni di Palazzo Grassi", Venice 1997.

M. De Angelis d'Ossat, F. Scoppola, *La contesa de Numi nelle collezioni di scultura antica a Palazzo Altemps*, Rome 1997.

PHOTOGRAPHS AND PLANS

The photographs are from the
archives of the Soprintendenza
Archeologica di Roma and are
by Eugenio Monti.

The plans of the palace
are from the archives of the
Soprintendenza Archeologica
di Roma and were redrawn
by Ludovico Bisi.

PALAZZO ALTEMPS

Text
Francesco Scoppola
and Stella Diana Vordemann

Translated by
Edward Steinberg

Translations of passages by
non-Italian authors are based
on Italian editions of their
works.

www.electaweb.it

Reprint 2002

©1997 Ministero per i Beni e le Attività Cuturali
Soprintendenza Archeologica di Roma
An editorial realization by Mondadori Electa S.p.a.

This book was printed for Mondadori Electa S.p.a.
at Tipografia La Piramide (Rome)
in the year 2002